People Who Live At The End
of Dirt Roads

People Who Live At The End *of* Dirt Roads

Lee Pitts
Illustrations by Don Dane

Fourth Edition

Text Copyright© 1995 by Lee Pitts
Illustration Copyright© 1995 by Don Dane

Inquiries regarding this book should be addressed to:
Lee Pitts
P.O. Box 616
Morro Bay, CA 93443

Designed by Mary Ellen Thompson
Edited by Dawn Valentine Hadlock
Cover art and illustrations by Don Dane
Published by Lee Pitts
Printed by Image Graphics, Paducah, KY

ISBN No. 0-9666334-1-5

For my wife, Diane,
with love and appreciation.

CONTENTS

Do you really want to know what is wrong with American society today?

Too many of our roads have been paved.

There's not a problem in America today—crime, education, drugs, the divorce rate—that could not be improved with more dirt roads.

THE GOLDEN AGE OF AMERICA

(PART ONE)

MANY OF THE ITEMS being sold at the farm sale were old and funny looking. Most of them didn't work and had only been kept around for sentimental reasons. In that regard, they were like the husbands who were now rummaging through what was left of four generations of a family farm.

The bidding was frantic on the Mason jars and jelly jugs that contained homemade sausage. They were bought by a restaurateur from the city. He probably did not want the sausage but would use the jars as cocktail glasses and serve four-dollar fruity drinks with umbrellas in them.

We all wanted the old quilts that somebody's grandmother had made. It seemed everybody slept better under a grandmother quilt. Was that a tear in the eye of the much-loved, antique bisque doll? She brought more money than the modern-day versions that wet, carry on conversation, and cry.

The auctioneer asked for bids on an old-fashioned phone, and one man stopped talking on his cellular long enough to place a bid. I even raised my hand on some old milk bottles in a wire basket. I can fondly remember when the milkman left some just like them on our front porch every other morning. You wouldn't dare leave *these* antiques on the porch though—they brought fifty dollars.

There were pewter cups and silver spoons—all purchased at the five-and-ten store when that meant pennies, not dollars. The dust flew as the dealers fought over a rare book with "Happy Birthday Tom" inscribed on the inside cover. I'd be willing to bet they didn't even know who Tom was.

Some of the furniture dated back to Chippendale and some of it went back to Sears and Roebuck. The buyers were discriminating. They all wanted the commode made out of "real wood," but the reproduction with its factory dents and artificial aging only brought a buck. The particleboard reproduction would never be an antique—it wouldn't last that long.

After the auctioneer was through selling the household contents, he passed the auctioneer's gavel to a real estate broker to sell the homestead. He was then joined on the front porch by the present owner—a banker. The banker unlocked the front door and swung it wide for all the "Looky-Lous" to enter. I bet the previous owners had never felt a need to lock their front door out here in the country.

The house was in a sad state. It was an old Victorian with high ceilings and windowpanes, the kind that little kids pressed their faces against waiting for daddy to come in from the fields. There were knife nicks on the doorjamb where the family's growth had been chronicled. Somehow it didn't feel proper being in that house when nobody was home. I needed some fresh air.

I walked around the old home place. There was a license plate collection on the garage wall and a few gaps in the row of poplar trees that formed a windbreak. The only thing sprouting in what used to be a garden was a stick that probably had held up a radish package. There were imprints of tiny feet fossilized in the concrete walkway. I wondered if they belonged to the child who had played in the tree house in the dying eucalyptus tree. Berries grew on an old rock fence that was falling down. We never build fences like that anymore it seems. The corral posts were still solid and so was the barn. The outhouse was falling down, though it had long ago served its intended purpose.

The homestead was purchased by a corporate farmer who will no doubt bulldoze the farmhouse or use it to keep his fertilizer dry.

The rusty old farm implements were the last things to sell. No, that's not correct, they didn't actually sell. The auctioneer gave them to a salvage operator just for hauling them away.

When the auction was over, there was nothing of value left behind—or was there?

THE GOLDEN AGE OF AMERICA

(PART TWO)

I COULDN'T GO TO AN auction and not buy anything. The problem was that I didn't know what I had just bought at the farm sale, although I knew it was valuable. The auctioneer had called it a "brank," and I had a feeling the device had been an old family heirloom. Supposedly it was to be used on scolding women who had the irritating habit of talking too much. It sat on the subject's head, and when she wagged her tongue, it moved a lever that forced spines into the top of her head. I gave thirty dollars for it in a spirited bidding battle!

I paid the cashier and dodged the throng of henpecked husbands who begged me to sell my brank to them. Hurrying to my car, I couldn't wait to get home and show the new purchase to my wife.

The farm sale was just outside a small town that I had visited many years before. I remembered the town because I had once filled up with a whole tank of gas there before I realized I didn't have my wallet or credit card. The proprietor said, "No big deal, just mail a check when you get home."

I pulled into the familiar gas station. I was feeling pretty sad anyway after attending the farm sale, but when I drove in and saw the boarded-up station, I felt even worse. Somebody had even removed the pumps.

I'm sure it had been the small town everyone makes jokes about. There wasn't any crime in the streets because there weren't any streets. An evening of culture consisted of sitting on the front porch and watching the sun go down. The only thing on television after ten at night was the test pattern.

I was glad to see the town wasn't completely deserted. An old dog watched the cars file past as they were going home from the farm sale. Some entrepreneurial soul had bought one of the old houses and fixed it up into a bed-and-breakfast in an attempt to attract "the beautiful people" from the city. The broken-down picket fence out front suggested that the idea hadn't worked out very well.

I suppose it would be generalizing to say that once upon a time this town had represented everything that was good during "America's Golden Age." When a funeral passed, everybody in town knew who was in the box. The close-knit townsfolk lived in harmony. There were no traffic jams, and the only form of pollution was a flatulent horse. There wasn't any street crime, and yes, they did have a street. I'm sure the kids still said they hated the one-room schoolhouse, but I bet they wanted to go back in September.

I'm sure some of the local boys made good and moved away to a better neighborhood where their kids swam in swimming pools instead of swimming holes and played on baseball diamonds instead of cow pastures. Other families had been forced to move away. The farm sale I had just attended was a brutal reminder of that.

Car after car hurried past me, filled with antiques and relics and broken dreams. It seems we value the relics but not the society that produced them. Middle America is vanishing. These small towns along the way either flourished and grew into a city with all its problems, or they died. If enough families move away, a small town dies. If enough small towns die, the heart of a nation is destroyed.

I wonder what the antiques from our generation will be, or will anything of our making last that long? Surely a generation without a past can't have much of a future.

A Man of Letters

IF YOUR HOME WAS in the path of an advancing fire or raging floodwaters and you had to escape and could only take one thing with you, what would it be? Cats, dogs, and kids would probably be first on your list, although not necessarily in that order. Along with my wife, I know what I would take with me—a little bundle of letters wrapped with a frayed piece of yarn.

You remember personal letters, don't you? They were how we used to communicate before the advent of car phones, E-mail, and fax machines. No, I am not referring to those letters from Ed McMahon informing you that you may have already won ten million dollars. I am not talking about letters that are addressed, "Dear Patron," "Dear Occupant," or my favorite, "Dear Valued Customer." If you are so valued, how come they didn't take the time to write you a real letter?

The letters I cherish are the kind that begin, "How are you? I am fine." They are old letters from a now-deceased grandparent, a word of advice from an older brother or sister at graduation, and the most cherished of all—those first love letters. I am talking about the kind of letters that made going to the mailbox the highlight of each day.

Letters are literature. Hemingway wrote some great ones, and some of Mark Twain's best writing was found in letters to his friends. It seems to me that letter writing has become a lost art. That's a shame because the feeling one got from writing a letter was almost as good as the elation one felt at receiving one. When you finished, you couldn't wait to get your masterpiece to the mailbox. In writing a letter you actually gave someone your time, your most valued possession.

Instead of sitting down and writing a personal note these days, a person will spend an hour and a half in a card store looking for just the right sentiment. They could have written it themselves and saved two dollars. Those greeting cards are beautiful, but I have never seen one as pretty as a hand-drawn picture or a thank-you note from a nephew or a niece.

Admittedly, there are some personal letters that fall into the junk-mail category, such as "Dear John" letters and the Xeroxed letters you receive at Christmas from your very rich and important friends. This is cheating. These are no more "real" letters than those computer-generated ones the IRS sends out. I don't save any letter with a fancy letterhead or with those small initials at the bottom that indicate it was written by someone other than the person who signed it. Important people dictate letters because they can use words they don't know how to spell.

Letters are what journalists call "hard copy." They exist. They are not like a phone call that vanishes when you hang up. Letters can be passed around, reread, and saved. They can be steamed over a teakettle, read, and resealed. Letters are prized possessions, and if you want to spend an enjoyable afternoon next time it rains, go find your little bundle of letters and read a few. See what I mean?

I noticed recently that the post office is advertising on television to drum up new business. If they really wanted to sell more stamps, I think they should start a letter-writing campaign. Why not encourage school kids to write one letter a week to a friend, relative, or pen pal? Besides helping out the post office, it just might teach more kids how to read and write.

If you are ever in a quandary as to what to give a person for a birthday, graduation, or other special occasion, take the time to write a letter. Believe me, it will mean more than any trinket you buy and will certainly last longer.

TALKING FENCES

IN A PERFECT WORLD, there would be far fewer fences, I think.

I don't know what the study of fences is called, but I do know you can learn a lot about people by the kind of fence they live behind. You can tell if people enjoy life or want to hide behind a wall in their own little world, not even wanting to catch a glimpse of someone else's. By looking at a fence, you can tell if the government paid for it or which neighbor got stuck with the bill. (When a neighbor fails to share the cost, they always get the ugly side of the fence. There is no ugly side when the government pays for it.)

Recently I made a journey from the inner city to the country just studying the fences and walls that enclose and divide us. In the heart of the inner city, I was fenced in everywhere I went by mean brick walls and wrought-iron, bulletproof barriers. In each case, the message was the same—"this is mine and that is yours." Often the message was punctuated with a Doberman or a dash of electric current. It was easy to see that many people lived in fear behind their fences. Often the grotesquely ugly fences were decorated by the angry art of graffiti impressionists.

Some fences said "stay out" more politely than others. In the middle of the inner city, surrounded by iron and brick, I spotted the fence of an optimist. A cute little white-picket fence said ever so nicely, "This may be mine, but I hope you enjoy looking at it." Right across the street was a six-foot-high, chain-link fence with concertina wire on top. I couldn't tell if it protected a school or a prison.

It was often difficult to determine if the fences were keeping people on the outside from coming in or keeping people behind the fences from coming out. Fences separated neighbor from neighbor. They separated Chinatown from Little Italy and Spanish Harlem. Rich people were protected by thick walls mounted with surveillance cameras—television fences!

The farther one got out into the country, the fewer fences there were. The personality of the fences seemed to change, too. In small-town America, the concertina wire was replaced by broken-down, backyard, board fences that neighbors have been talking over for generations. Oh, the stories those fences could tell!

In the country, there was even an occasional rock wall. Those fences spoke of skilled craftsmen, rocky pastures, and a bygone era when a person could take the time to build something beautiful. I wonder, does it say something about our society that these fences are falling down and no one knows how to fix them?

Out in the country, when I saw the miles of barbed wire that surround our world, I could only relate to my own experience— of all the blisters and the bloody cuts it took to build those fences. Can you imagine all the work it took to fence the West?

What do these barbed-wire fences of ours tell us? They are strong enough to stop a tumbling tumbleweed but not strong enough to hold back the younger generation from leaving the land. On barbed-wire fences, the bottom wire is off the ground where newspapers with the ugly headlines of the day can blow on by without notice. Raccoons and squirrels scurry underneath, deer and antelope jump over, and grass grows beneath. An occasional wooden post has taken root, just like the people who live behind these "see-through" fences.

I suppose fences are necessary; but after studying the matter, I have come to the conclusion that the best kind of fences are those that you don't notice.

CHOICES

A FEW YEARS AGO, when the service was being taken out of the local service station, I asked with a flushed face, "Why is the door to the rest room locked? Can I have the key?" I pleaded in desperation.

"That courtesy is being eliminated," I was told by the new proprietor. Along with washing my windows and checking my oil, rest rooms had been discontinued. I told the new owner he'd go broke and that I wouldn't be back—but he didn't, and I did. After all, his gas was cheaper.

The nice lady in the bakery used to ask, "How may I help you?" Now a stranger tells me to "Take a number." Somehow the cinnamon rolls don't taste as good, but I still go there—out of habit, I guess.

We don't have one of those new, huge, discount supermarkets in my small town yet. Out of curiosity, I did go into one in a neighboring city. I had to bag my own groceries, and a computer scanner read the price tags and told me the price. The only human I saw was the poor soul who took my money. She was probably making minimum wage. The groceries sure were cheaper than at my hometown grocery store where the nice checkers made union wages. Their costs are higher because they gave the neighbor kid a decent box-boy job and allowed a mother of two, whose husband had left her, a chance to make a decent living instead of being on welfare. I wonder where I will shop in the future when one of those super stores moves in and my little town goes discount?

It upsets me terribly that one of the banks I do business with was just bought out by the Japanese. My blood boiled when I heard on *60 Minutes* that the Japanese had bought up 60 percent of downtown Houston and 50 percent of L.A. a few years ago, but I had to admit to myself that I did own a Japanese car once. I wonder if those extra five miles to the gallon were worth it?

My wife and I worry about what is in the food we eat and whether or not the modern-day additives are unhealthy or could cause cancer. We gave up on growing a garden and baking bread years ago. It was just too much work.

I have to admit that it bothers me to see middle-aged men in the city park drinking from jugs hidden in brown paper bags. Why don't they get a job or fade away where I can't see them? I feel sorry for them, but I know that when a new computer comes along and can save us from hiring two new people in our own little office, we would probably buy it.

It disturbs me to see a greedy rancher sell out to a big-city developer who wants to build ocean-front condos on what was a beautiful cattle ranch. I wonder, though, if someone offered me $20,000 an acre, would I take it?

I drive in the fast lane on the three-lane freeway to get ahead of everyone else, but everyone else is thinking the same thing. That is why there is nobody in the slow lane. Sometimes I wonder if I wouldn't get there faster going slower.

We all seem to be overweight in this country. We blame it on the food, but maybe it's because we don't work very hard anymore. Have you noticed that the less hard work a person does, the more money he makes? Is it better to be rich and unhealthy or to have calloused hands, an empty checkbook, and a good heart?

In suburbia we hire landscapers to do our yards now instead of a local schoolboy. After all, the landscaper doesn't leave strips of grass unmowed or weeds unpulled. Then we hope and pray that our own kids don't get on another kind of grass because they have too much time on their hands.

I understand that both parents must work nowadays so they can give their kids everything they want and need. Maybe what they want and need is to be raised by their parents instead of Child Care Incorporated.

They say the quality of life is deteriorating in this country. I say you get what you pay for.

THE FIX-IT MAN

BENNY WAS A Japanese handyman who worked for my grandfather in his furniture store. He could fix anything—toilets, tractors, stoves, marriages, window blinds—anything. No one ever had to wait for a part to come either. Benny had one of everything in the back of his truck. That was my job, to find the part. He would be under a heater and tell me to go to the truck and get a "watchamacallit." If by some chance I couldn't find the right part, he would make one with his calloused hands. Today we'd probably call him a consultant, but I always thought of Benny as a genius. He knew how to do things.

We went out on a lot of false alarms. The elderly ladies in town would call up and say, "Benny, my washing machine doesn't sound right." Benny would go out to their house and listen to their wringer washer, which sounded just fine. Of course, there was no charge, just a couple cups of coffee. The lonely ladies just wanted a little company or maybe they wanted Benny to look at their sick dog or cat. He knew a lot about animals, too.

Once every six years, a certain lady would call about her stove. All she really wanted was to have the floor cleaned out behind it.

That was my job, too. Benny still drank the coffee, but we charged her plenty. Even though Benny never got rich, I think he did all right. He always had enough money to buy me a chili cheese dog from Aphis down at the truck stop.

Benny was widely known for telling stories. The women liked the ones slightly off-color. They would get red in the face and say, "Oh, Benny, you shouldn't say that. Do you know any more?"

Benny could tell a housewife how to take the oil stain out of her carpet in six different languages. He knew how to patch up sinks and family squabbles. He could take a drunk off the bottle and lift a bum off the floor. I had seen him do it.

Benny had a small farm at the end of a dirt road where every year he grew a wonderful garden. He used to try and see how hot he could grow chili peppers. He would use them in the wonderful Mexican food he cooked. His specialty, though, was sweet corn. Around the dinner table all over town, folks would sit down to sweet corn that they had just purchased at Mitch's Garden Market. They would say, "This is the best corn I ever ate. It must be Benny's." The townsfolk just felt a little better knowing that Benny grew it.

It was quite an honor for me to ride shotgun with Benny in his truck all over town as ladies waved and dogs followed. I'm sure Benny had his faults, but I can't remember any. I never heard him argue and never heard a bad word said about the kind and gentle man.

I'm sure I asked too many questions of Benny as a child, but he knew important things. The weatherman on the radio would say it was going to be partly sunny; then Benny would look up into a clear sky and see the blackbirds starting to flock on the telephone wires. "Looks like rain to me," he'd say. Sure enough, we'd get two inches of moisture. Benny understood. He had a knack for seeing things as they were and doing things as they ought to be done.

I don't know how much schooling Benny had. But I do know that after the Japanese bombed Pearl Harbor and when the government started sending the rest of the Japanese-Americans in my town to detention camps, Benny didn't get mad at America. He enlisted in the army of the country that would have taken everything he owned if he had stayed home. Benny never talked about the war, but I was told that he served with distinction and won his share of medals.

They will never put a sign up on the edge of our town that says, "Benny Taketa lived here," but our town was a lot better off because he did.

Pardon me for doing all this reminiscing, but when I look around and see all the things in this world that could be fixed with a little common sense, I think of Benny. Common sense these days is not so common. Neither was Benny.

PEOPLE WHO LIVE
AT THE END OF DIRT ROADS

DO YOU REALLY WANT to know what is wrong with American society today?

Too many of our roads have been paved.

There's not a problem in America today—crime, education, drugs, the divorce rate—that could not be improved with more dirt roads.

Dirt roads build character. People who live at the end of dirt roads know that life is much more enjoyable when taken at a slower pace. They know that life can be dirty, boring, and can jar you right down to your teeth at times. They also have a greater appreciation for what's waiting at the end of the bumpy ride—their home, their kids, a frisky dog, and a loving spouse.

We wouldn't have near the trouble with our educational system today if more kids still lived at the end of dirt roads and had to take the bus to school. In the old days, buses usually wouldn't go down dirt roads, so the kids had to walk to the bus stop. In doing so, they got a lot more exercise than they would sitting in front of television for hours on end. Kids often learned more on the bus than they did in the classroom, too. Bus riders seldom became social misfits. Kids learned how to get along, how to make conversation, and often did their homework on the bus. Usually, the last kid to get off the bus at the end of the route was the smartest kid in the class.

At the end of dirt roads youngsters soon learned that bad words tasted like Ivory Soap. An older brother or sister took real good care of a younger sibling because often they were the only ones to play with—or to blame things on. The children knew that play time couldn't commence until the chores were done; but they would secretly tell you that when the chores were done, so was a lot of the real fun. Bottle feeding the calves, collecting eggs, and feeding the horse wasn't really work, at least not to a country kid.

There was less crime in our streets when most of them were dirt. Criminals just didn't walk down two miles of dirt road to rob or rape, because if they did, they were apt to be welcomed by five barking dogs and a double-barrel shotgun. People peddling vitamin supplements and religion stayed away in droves. There were no drive-by shootings either.

We had much better values when the roads were worse. Grown-ups didn't cherish their cars more than their kids. Country folks didn't drive $50,000 foreign cars down roads that were like corrugated iron. Instead, they drove pickup trucks that pleaded in dust on the tailgate, "Please wash me!" but no one ever did. Why bother? It would just get dirty again.

People were much more courteous in the days of dirt. Drivers didn't tailgate, because if they did, they would choke on your dust or get a rock through their windshield. Dirt roads taught patience.

Fancy folks didn't use hair spray or mousse gel in their hair in the days of dirt roads. If they did, by the time they got to the end of a road, their thirty-five-dollar haircut would be a sticky, gooey, filthy mess. Butch wax was bad enough.

Most paved roads led to a dead end. Dirt roads, on the other hand, most likely ended at a fishing creek or a favorite swimming hole. At the end of a dirt road, there was no need to arm your alarm or lock your car, unless it was to keep the neighbor from filling it with zucchini.

Dirt roads were much more environmentally friendly, too. You just didn't hop in your car and deplete the ozone layer to run to town and get a quart of milk. Instead, you went outside and milked the cow. You walked down to the end of the driveway to get the mail—usually catalogs from which you ordered everything from china cups to calico. If it rained and the road was washed out, you just stayed home, maybe even had a family conversation. Remember those?

At the end of a dirt road, there has always been extra income when a city dude got his car stuck and you had to pull him out. Usually you received a dollar or two; always, you got a new friend.

Now many of our roads have been paved over and some call it progress. Where do these roads lead? Mostly to trouble, I'd say.

This country was a lot better off when most of our people lived at the end of dirt roads.

MY KIND OF TOWN

I LIKE SMALL TOWNS. I am a sucker for towns with a sign at the city limits that proudly proclaims to be the home of someone or something. I recently saw a sign for a small town outside Minneapolis. The faded sign read, "Home of the 1991 Grand Champion Ham at the State Fair." I have always regretted that I didn't spend some time in that town of ham fame. It sounded like such a nice place.

There's a sign I saw in Strasburg, North Dakota, that proudly claims to be the "Home of Lawrence Welk." I liked the town a whole lot better than I ever did the *Lawrence Welk Show*. A picture of Rex Allen in the McDonalds in Willcox, Arizona, reminded me that this favorite town of mine was his birthplace. That's quite an honor, I would think, to be enshrined at the local McDonalds.

A person doesn't necessarily have to be good to have his or her name in lights at the city limits. Fort Sumner, New Mexico, claims Billy the Kid as a resident, and I am told that some towns even claim politicians.

Perhaps the best thing that can be said about a person is that their hometown is proud of them. I sure would be honored someday if I had my own billboard in my hometown. I suppose that is asking too much though—after all, it already is the "Lemon Capital of the World."

I like small towns that are the "World Capital" of something. Wenatchee, Washington, which has clean air, clean streets, and clean people, proudly claims to be the "Apple Capital of the World." I like apples and Wenatchee, and I think they deserve each other.

I had a great time in Las Vegas once. No, it was Las Vegas, New Mexico, not Sin City, Nevada. I like Columbus, Montana, better than the bigger one in Ohio. I'd rather vacation in Miami, Oklahoma, as opposed to the one in Florida.

Any list of my all-time favorite towns would have to include Sterling, Colorado. A nice man there once let me in the Elk's Club on a very cold night, and I'm not even a member. Prairie Du Chien, Wisconsin, is about the prettiest place I've ever been. I was there in leaf season, and the birches were yellow, the maples were scarlet, the sumac was purple, and the people were red, white, and blue. Tillamook, Oregon, the town that gave cheese a good name, would be a close second for prettiest-place honors.

I have not traveled in the East as much as the West but I have discovered some lovely towns back there. One of my favorites is

Lancaster, Pennsylvania. It is the home of the largest stockyards east of the Mississippi, and the people there aren't ashamed to tell the world. It takes a big town to do that. I enjoyed Brush, Colorado, a whole lot more than New York City. New York seems so far removed from anywhere else.

Small towns have character. I once left a jacket with money in the pocket in Alpine, Texas, and both the cash and the jacket got back home before I did. Mountain Home, Idaho, is as good as it sounds. I think it would be a great place to raise a family.

Sheridan, Wyoming, is an "All-American City," or so says the sign at the city limits. I slept there in the same motel where two other All-Americans had previously stayed—Will Rogers and Buffalo Bill. If I can't have my own billboard in my hometown some day, I hope they at least put up a sign at the motel in Soap Lake, Washington, that says, "Lee Pitts slept here."

I like towns where the church building, not the video arcade, is still the center of social activity. I like towns where you can buy a pair of work gloves and a canned ham in the same store, but the store is not the size of three football fields. If I address a letter to a friend in Pie Town, New Mexico, and it gets there without a street address, then that's my kind of town. I like a town where the cemetery is well cared for, the church bells still ring (and can still be heard), and people still pull over for funeral processions.

There are still some towns I would love to visit, and hope to someday. In my travels, I want to visit Rustic, Colorado; Equality, Illinois; Opportunity, Montana; and Triumph, Louisiana.

I have mostly met America at her coffee shops. I have shared potato soup with a roustabout in Shamrock, Texas, and Mexican food with the Indians in Gallup, New Mexico. I think the best restaurant meal I ever had in my life was in a coffee shop in Yachats, Oregon.

Yes, I consider myself a world traveler. I have been to Moscow (the one in Idaho), and I have stayed in the finest hotels in both Belgrade and Glasgow (Montana). I have been to Paris, California, and Peru, Kansas, and I'd have to say that country folks everywhere—from Hermiston, Oregon, to DeRidder, Louisiana—are pretty much the same the world over.

SAVE THE BURGER

AMERICA IS SAVING itself from itself. Nowhere is this more evident than in the rebirth of the American hamburger.

In the 1940s, a nation came home from "The Big War" to her hamburger stands. America went on her first date in a 1950 Chevy to the local Dairy Freeze. Sweethearts shared a burger and literally spawned the baby-boom generation. Perhaps historians shall one day say that this hamburger generation was truly our Golden Age.

This era was followed by twenty-five dark years in the annals of hamburger history. The baby boomers grew up and the old values weren't good enough anymore. The turbulent sixties was a decade of decadence. There was civil unrest in America's streets and gastrointestinal unrest in her body. The old Dairy Freeze on the corner was replaced by a fast-food chain that didn't care if you liked your burger rare, medium, or well. You couldn't take out the pickles because they were all chopped up and hidden between three pieces of chemically preserved bread and two beef patties. They tasted more like cow patties.

Big business decided that we needed a break today—that we wanted convenience wrapped in plastic. We no longer needed napkins because the hamburgers were no longer messy. The chains threw anything and everything at us as long as it was fast. One chain even served us kangaroo burgers—remember those?

It wasn't always like that. A&W Root Beer had a burger for everybody in the fifties. There was the Poppa, Momma, Teen, and Baby Burger. But then the family was forgotten in the sixties. We went macho with the Big Mac, the Whopper, the Dude, the Super Burger, and the Big Boy. No wonder women stopped eating hamburgers and started eating tofu.

In the "Me Generation" of the seventies, people ate only to make a statement. Grown-up hippies were eating things like yogurt and bean curd, and drinking wine coolers. I have a sneaky suspicion, though, that behind closed doors they were still eating hamburgers—about forty billion a year, to be exact. Then in the eighties, yuppies started doing strange things to their burgers. There were taco burgers, Cantonese burgers, pizza burgers, flambéed burgers, and flame-broiled burgers.

Lately, it seems that America is reinventing the good old hamburger. The fast-food joints have gone back to old-fashioned hamburgers with real lettuce, tomatoes, mustard, mayonnaise, and American cheese. There are even full-sized pickles that you can take out and throw away if you choose. Recently, I actually had to wait a few minutes while they cooked my hamburger—and you know what? I didn't mind waiting at all.

Yes, America is rebuilding on a foundation of old-fashioned values. My faith has been restored. Napkins and "Old-fashioned Hamburgers" are back. The restoration of America is underway. Who knows, maybe next they'll put the milk back in milk shakes.

KISS

WHY IS IT THAT IN conversation with one's horse or one's dog, we use simple, one-syllable words like "come," "sit," or "speak," but when we talk to fellow human beings, we feel compelled to use multisyllable palaver that none of us understand?

For example, on a delayed plane trip recently, we were offered "a complimentary beverage service." We'd have been just as thrilled if the flight attendant had simply said, "Free drinks!" When the plane ride got so bumpy that my "complimentary beverage" spilled itself in my lap, the pilot said that we were experiencing "some minor turbulence." Maybe *he* was experiencing minor turbulence, but *I* was being tossed around like a green salad. It was a real Maalox moment.

It's not just those folks with their heads in the air who use big words—all of us are guilty. On the plane that day, I read a realtor magazine that had been left behind by the previous occupant of my seat. It urged realtors to watch their language: Instead of using the word "commission," realtors were urged to refer to their fair share as a "professional fee." It seems that the word "price" is a real turnoff, and the words "total investment" can make a two-thousand-dollar-a-month mortgage payment sound much better.

Bloated bureaucrats also use bloated words. A recent congressional report on the defense budget seemed to be written in code. Dead people were referred to as "collateral damage," bullets were "kinetic energy penetrators," an invasion was a "predawn vertical insertion," and a bomb was referred to as a "peacemaker." That, to me, is a counter-factual proposal (bald-faced lie).

Recently my wife received a postcard in the mail from her doctor advising her that it was time for her "comprehensive physiological and multiphasic health screening." I guess that makes it easier for the doctor to charge $150 an hour. When she climbed the vertical access facility (stairs) to the doctor's office, she found that the furniture had been removed to facilitate "office landscaping"—and they weren't talking about plants.

I would have thought that the plain-speaking livestock industry would have avoided such snobbishness, but just the other day I heard a slaughterhouse being referred to as a "destructuring facility." I suppose it was for upwardly mobile bovines.

I shouldn't cast stones; after all, the writing profession seems to control the market on gobbledygook. I was asked recently by a magazine to "generate some text for text-processing analysis." I wonder if it pays the same as just plain writing?

There are reasons why people use fat words when skinny ones will do. It makes them feel superior and proves to be much more profitable. You wouldn't think of paying fifteen dollars for a plate of noodles, but call it "fettucine" and it sounds like a "total investment." The same is true with coffee, which I have never liked. I tried to tell this to a friend recently, explaining that I didn't really like the taste of coffee.

"Ah, but this is not coffee," he said with a snobbish tone, "this is cappuccino."

So I took a sip, savored the unique nutty taste, and then spat it out. It tasted just like coffee to me.

In talking or writing, I always try to remember just one word—KISS. It stands for "Keep It Simple, Stupid."

HOMESICK

THE CORPORATE LAWYER looked out the window of his twelfth-story condominium and saw air that wasn't fit to breathe, gridlocked streets, and homeless people warming themselves on steam that belched from below. The city dweller assumed that's how the whole world looked. The urbanite saw no birds or fish and thought the entire animal kingdom was endangered. The only animals visible were pets and they were locked up, although the criminals that stalked the city streets were not.

This civilized resident of New York City commuted to Washington, D.C., on business and vacationed in Atlantic City. From these extensive travels, he assumed that people were the same the world over. America was like a golden triangle—there was New York, L.A., and Disney World, with nothing of any consequence in the middle. You could get lost out there in the heartland.

Something is changing in his world, though—something profound. America is moving. The U-Hauls are headed home, beyond the sprawl. For the first time in California's history, more thirty and forty year olds left the state than moved in. Moving-van companies report that seven out of ten families leaving the big cities are moving to less urbanized areas.

It's not just the city residents getting back to basics—businesses are boomeranging back to the country also. Most of our great American corporations started out in small towns, grew up, and then moved to the big city. Just like the country kids, you couldn't keep them down on the farm. But guess who is coming home to the hinterlands? Texaco, JCPenney, even Exxon left New York for Irving, Texas. Every corporation that can do its business someplace cheaper is migrating. Wal-Mart, the nation's largest retailer, is located in Bentonville, Arkansas, and Phillips Petroleum can be found in Bartlesville, Oklahoma.

With computers, faxes, and overnight delivery, it is no longer necessary to live in New York to be in touch with the real world. Boise is just as good, or North Platte, or Grand Junction. Besides, New York never knew much about the real world anyway.

Even blow-dried, 1980s-type, money managers (the ones who escaped jail sentences) are moving to the country—and not just for the fishing. States with big populations are barely able to pay their bills, so they are raising all sorts of new taxes. In an effort to keep some of their own money, people are moving out. Realtors call it "moving down." Those who have tried it say it is moving up.

Americans are getting cabin fever. Big-city dwellers are trying to unload their row houses, condos, and their $1,500-a-month mortgages. They are tired of schools and panhandlers that promise to work but don't. They are tired of muggers and corrupt politicians, both after the same thing.

Along with this change of address comes a new attitude. The last yuppie died in 1990. (They were bores anyway.) They could no longer afford the latest hip haircut because theirs was a false economy. So now they are trading in their gold cards for library cards. They had to give up their country club membership and decided to move to the real country where you can actually get a tee time and don't need a home equity loan to pay the initiation fee.

As America moves back home, we will be seeing fewer Japanese cars and more American-made trucks; fewer Gucci loafers and more Justin Ropers. Americans who have been eating tofu and sun-dried tomatoes and drinking expensive water will finally taste it and say, "This stuff tastes awful." As Americans come home, they will rediscover homemade cooking, free parking, fresh air, the great outdoors, and their own children. The shopping mall and video arcade were never proper places to raise children anyway.

Americans are rediscovering what those of us who live in the country have known all along: You can't send down roots in soil that has been paved over in cement and asphalt.

IMPROVEMENT, INC.

IF YOU ARE EVER TEMPTED to buy something that is "New and Improved," take my word for it, the item will probably cost more and will not work as well as the tried-and-true version.

Take my new lawn mower, for example . . . please. It has so many new safety gadgets on it that every time I want to empty the grass catcher, I have to shut the engine off. This means I have to pull the starter cord thirty-seven times every time I want to mow my lawn. I suppose the idea is that you won't end up in the hospital with a severed hand . . . just a sprained back.

Some tools just weren't meant to be improved upon. One of the hottest-selling Christmas gifts for many years now has been the electric screwdriver. It works great—until the screw actually meets some resistance, such as putting a screw through some hard wood or metal. Then you have real problems! Don't worry, though, because the electric screwdriver can then be locked into a manual mode where it can be used just like a regular screwdriver. Why not just use a regular screwdriver to begin with?

I see they have a new electric wrench coming on the market just in time for this Christmas—same principle—probably more batteries. I think I'll pass.

Hardware stores are full of "New and Improved" products like the leaf blower. They have sold millions of these things and all the gadgets do is blow the leaves from your yard to your neighbor's yard. Of course, this inspires your neighbor to rush right down to the hardware store and buy one so he can blow the leaves back to your place. Whatever happened to the broom? Some nut is probably trying to motorize it, I suppose.

Car companies are famous for improving things. I had a flat tire a month ago, and for the first time I discovered the miniature spare tire hiding in my trunk. I guess the car companies figure they are saving money by not giving you a real tire for the $20,000 you paid for your new car. I had my wife put on the minispare and it went flat within two miles! I ruined the minispare, but as far as I'm concerned, it was no great loss.

The phone company is always trying to improve their service. Now they have something known as "call waiting" that enables someone you didn't want to speak with in the first place to call you in the middle of your favorite television show and put you on *hold*. I hate that! AT&T keeps calling me and trying to sell me on some special plan they have that will "save me money." If it's better and will save me money, then why aren't they already doing it? Why do they need my permission?

I am all for safety and the environment, but I do have a feeling that some government commission of idiots sits in a room and dreams up packaging to drive us all crazy. My four-year-old niece can open the safety cap on a bottle of pills, but my wife can't. How about those plastic things that hold a six-pack of beer together? I suppose the plastic is more politically correct than the old-fashioned cardboard cartons, but now I have to cut the plastic rings because a duck hung himself in one—at least that's what they said on television.

I asked for a sharper knife in a restaurant last week and was refused because I might cut myself and sue the establishment. By the way, don't remove the safety hood on your new can opener or all lawsuits are off!

Just the other day I bought a can of bug spray that I had used in the past with good results. The new-and-improved can said it was more environmentally friendly than the old one. Maybe so, but they made the spray so safe it doesn't work. I went back to the store to buy the good stuff and guess what—they don't make it anymore.

Some things don't need improving, and I wish people would quit trying.

THE INVISIBLE MAN

HE LIVES IN A REST HOME NOW, and that is mostly what he does—rest. He's hibernating in the winter of his life. The sweet dreams are more enjoyable than the reality. Like the home he didn't want to leave, time and the seasons have destroyed his foundation. The walls are crumbling and the paint has long since faded. He receives few visitors, even the life-insurance salesmen stay away. He is growing old, and old age isn't very popular these days.

In his day he was one cool dude. He has told the nurses countless times about the night he dressed up in his twelve-dollar suit, splashed on some Palmer's Toilet Water, cruised in his 1921 Model T, and picked up his gal to go dancing to the tunes of Kitten on the Keys.

He can barely see out of his thick glasses now, but that is okay. He's seen it all anyway. He remembers a time when a dollar was still worth a quarter and service went with the service charge. He lived during a time when the merchandise outlasted the payments, horsepower had something to do with horses, and the powder room was outside.

Like most senior citizens, he likes to tell anybody who will listen about "the good old days." "I could buy a pound of steak for a dime in the good old days," he is fond of saying. What he doesn't tell you is that he had to work half a day to earn the dime.

He shuffles with a cane, has brown spots on his hands, and sports a shock of gray hair on top of his head. But this remarkable man made the transition from a twelve-party-line crank telephone to the computer age. He went from wringer washers, three-cent stamps, one-room schools, and horse-drawn buggies to the atom bomb and a man on the moon. Can you imagine?

He is occasionally grumpy, but there is a kindness in his heart behind the rough exterior. There is also a gleam in his eye—or is it the salty moisture of a tear? He has arthritis, you know.

He would be the first to tell you that age itself is no guarantee of quality. All antiques are not priceless, and he was no angel. He owned a twenty-gallon still during Prohibition, but he was also on the victory train when it rolled through town following the First World War.

I don't know if he saved too little or just lived too long, but his belongings all fit in the dresser by his bed. Tucked away out of sight, he is but one of our generation's invisible people— unseen by the rest of us.

Yet these invisible men and women found a cure for polio, and they taught the world how to farm. They built our nation's interstates, her trestles, and her dams. They fought on foreign beaches. They built the greatest democracy the world has ever known.

He is at that golden age when he finally knows some of the answers to the game of life . . . but nobody takes the time to ask him the questions.

All Fall Down

THE PROBLEM WITH THIS country is not that our kids are spoiled, the inflation rate is high, or our politicians are crooked—all that is nothing new. The real problem is that our barns are falling down.

In my file of yesterdays, some of my fondest memories are of the hours I spent in our barn. When I was a kid, the barn was a place where I could build things out of scrap lumber. Most of the time I really didn't know what I was building until it was finished.

For the man of the house, the barn was a place to get away from the woman of the house, maybe even hide a bottle. For the farm wife, it was a place to send things, like old mattresses, retired furniture, bratty kids, or grumpy husbands. When she wanted you out of the house, the barn was where you went to pout. But you didn't really mind going.

Nobody builds barns anymore. Oh sure, they build ugly metal things and call them "farm shops." Modern-day corporate agriculturalists have an edifice complex—the bigger the better. They wouldn't think of building an old-fashioned wooden structure. Just as well—probably couldn't find anybody to build one anyway. But these modern-day enclosures aren't really barns, at least not of the dirt-floor variety.

In a real barn, you could look up through the roof and see the stars, or maybe they were the eyes of an old hoot owl who had taken up residence. The rafters were big, thick timbers hooked together without nails, notched and grooved. The barn door slid on overhead wheels and probably still does after all these years. A horseshoe still hangs above the door, not upside down though—that would let all the luck run out. If there were any windows in the barn, the glass was of the prism variety—the ripples and imperfections reflected the sun's rays into many splendid colors. Old license plates or an old green can of bag balm had been flattened and nailed to the wall to cover the holes and prevent drafts.

Most of the old barns were built when horsepower was provided by horses. Even after horses were replaced with Mustangs and Pintos, the barn still served as home to the mouser, the mud daubers who made their nests in the eaves, and the dog who had his private stash there. Give a dog a bone and it probably ended up buried in the barn. Newborn lambs were jailed inside with their reluctant mothers, sick animals were given shelter, and chickens laid their eggs there.

Old barns were great for storing things. We called it "junk" then, but now antique stores sell the stuff to city folk who call it "rustic." If we'd only known, we would have saved more of that stuff. Hay hooks with broken handles, an old scythe hanging from a square nail, and cobwebs adorned the barn walls. Often the family anvil is still to be found in the barn, nearly held in as high esteem as the family bible.

I collect old things found in barns. My prize possessions include an old can of Dr. J. H. McLean's Volcanic Oil Liniment for Man or Beast. The can said it would cure anything. Obviously it didn't. I also have an old wooden box that someone took the time to make. Must have taken at least a whole day to build this simple little box. Can you imagine the joy and pride that a project like that must bring? Can you imagine having the time?

It saddens me that most of these old barns are falling down. The "Mail Pouch" signs have long since faded from the roof, to be replaced by more colorful but less effective billboards. The weather-beaten shingles hang to a weakened skeleton, the wind trying to pry them loose. The roof is always the first to go, but the siding soon follows—taken by someone who wants to panel a den in their urban home or give a restaurant some rustic ambience.

I hope we make an effort to save some of these historic buildings. Like a cave painting or a pyramid, they reveal so much about the people who made them.

TAKE THIS JOB AND LOVE IT

YOU WOULD THINK THAT with computers, car phones, and voice mail, American workers are becoming far more productive. Right? Oh sure, more people are employed these days, but fewer of them are actually working.

We have lost our respect in this country for people who work hard: the carpenters, truck drivers, farmers, ranchers, mechanics, nurses, short-order cooks, grocery clerks, and mothers. We are told that more women have entered the workforce, probably to get out of the real dirty work at home. It seems that we want our children to be something better than just a "hard worker." "How I Became Rich Without Working" is the new bible of the baby-boom generation. Even the bearded man with the sign "Will work for food" doesn't really want to.

It is possible for teenagers today to graduate from college without ever having dug a ditch, mowed a lawn, thrown a paper route, picked fruit, or worked in a car wash. How can people like that call themselves educated? After graduation they are surprised to learn that being computer-game proficient doesn't guarantee a paycheck. They are forced to enter a job-training program so they'll know what kind of a job they are out of.

I recently heard a lady on a talk show who graduated three years ago with a fine arts degree. For three years she has been unable to find a job. Oh sure, there were jobs in the classified ads for cooks, gardeners, truck drivers, and people who knew how to do things, but none of them appealed to her. Besides, she wouldn't work for what they were willing to pay. She was especially mad because she was ineligible for unemployment compensation. It seems that she needed to have had a job once to be unemployed from. Pity. I could tell that being without work had destroyed that lady's dignity.

For some reason people think they are guaranteed a job in this country. The way I read it, we are only guaranteed life, liberty, and the pursuit of happiness. I never heard anything about a job. These people who are jobless are often the very same people who want to put roadblocks in front of businesses of any kind. They hate loggers, miners, ranchers, farmers, manufacturers—anybody who creates jobs. Yet they think their unemployment is somebody else's fault. I urge them to go start their own company in today's business climate if they think it's so easy.

We are spending increasing amounts of time and energy making things easier. Microwave meals, easy-care floors, and remote-control switches—anything to get out of work. I wonder, are we happier because of these conveniences? We have created all these things to get us out of work, and yet we, as a nation, have become overweight and stressed out. In our free time we have pursued material prosperity and searched for happiness in drugs, booze, faster cars, and expensive restaurants. We cocoon ourselves in our homes to protect us from people of lesser status, like those good folks who work for a living.

We are afraid of foreign competition, primarily because we don't like the thought of competing against people who still know how to work hard. However, going back to work is exactly what this country needs.

Real wealth is not produced by telemarketing. I recently heard a talk-show host refer to grain as a "low-value commodity." Ask a starving kid in Somalia who has the higher value, the farmer who produced the life-giving grain or the talk-show host. A logger is thought of as an unskilled rapist of the earth, but are you willing to give up your home, your use of toilet paper, or any of the other products made possible by the logger?

Real wealth is produced by making things, producing stuff, and, in the process, giving pride and meaning to a person's life. The feeling of coming home from a hard-day's work dirty, bone tired, and satisfied is the greatest feeling in the world. You just tend to eat and sleep better after a hard-day's work.

It seems to me that this country of ours would work a lot better if more of our citizens did.

TURNING INSIDE OUT

ARE YOU AN INSIDE PERSON or an outside person?

America seems to be moving indoors. New homes come complete with the barbecue pits on the inside now. If we want to know the weather, we turn on the television instead of poking our head out the door. We have made our pets so paranoid about the outdoors that they think it is only a place to go to the bathroom. We cover our canaries at night with a towel so they'll know when it's nighttime—the rest of us know by what's on the boob tube.

It used to be that sports were a good excuse to get outside, but now we are covering our stadiums with domes, our swimming pools with roofs, and our tennis courts with condominiums. We take vitamins because we don't get enough sun, and we get fat because we don't get enough exercise. To go for a walk nowadays, we get on a treadmill in the basement or go to a gym for some artificial exercise.

Our cars have become an extension of the home and are climatically controlled by computer to keep the temperature at 70°, even when it's 70° outside. Why not just roll down the window?

Mothers don't have to yell at the kids not to slam the screen door anymore because the children are inside playing Nintendo for hours on end. They don't want to go outside. Their $100 sneakers were only meant to be used on indoor, parquet, basketball floors, not asphalt, dirt, or concrete.

One reason that America has gone inside is that people who work inside—the doctors, lawyers, politicians, and such—generally make more money than those who work outdoors. Then the wealthy folks spend their money to make the inside of their homes and offices look like the outside. I have an acquaintance who spent $100 a square foot to build a home with a tree growing through the roof and flowers in an indoor atrium with an artificial creek running through it. He could have walked outside and had it all for free!

The outside comes with its own interior decorator, Mother Nature, and she doesn't charge nearly as much as the guy in the puce pumps.

I wonder, why should the fellow who sits at a computer designing a bridge be paid more than the bloke who risked his neck building the darn thing? I am told they now have computers that can actually simulate outside conditions, making it totally unnecessary for engineers and designers to ever go out into the real world. It seems to me that we are creating a society of weak, anemic, bug-eyed wimps afraid to go outside because their perms will get windblown, or they might come in contact with a bug. I can understand staying inside because of nasty weather, but that should be the only excuse, unless, of course, you live in the bad part of town.

There are those who would outlaw the outside if they could. They want to get rid of hunters, fishermen, and cowboys. They want to protect us from the outside, but it is the *inside* that is trying to kill us. Outdoorsmen are swarthy fellows and wise beyond books. Insiders are usually wimpy, white skinned, and microwaved.

The inside is artificial. I say we need more outdoor restaurants, more windows on the world, and more wildflowers. We need fewer indoor driving ranges, not to mention less insider trading and fewer inside deals. Come to think of it, I have never had a deal that I made outdoors go bad on me. I think we all tend to be a little more honest when we are outside. I suppose it's because we figure someone is watching us.

Rather than watch a football game on a Sunday afternoon, we ought to go outside and play one. Observing a squirrel scampering in the park is more entertaining than most television, and there are no commercials. The outside air cools the brain and turns the lungs pink, and we all know that food always tastes better when eaten out of doors. There's a whole big beautiful world outside, and more of it.

I don't like computer games, house cats, baseball under a roof, or indoor tanning salons. But then, I've always been sort of an outsider.

CRACKS IN THE CONCRETE

"Youth is such a wonderful thing. What a crime to waste it on children."

—George Bernard Shaw

I HAD ALWAYS THOUGHT I wanted to spend some time with kids, then one day I got my chance . . .

Last week I spent a very important day doing very important things, like collecting bird's feathers, listening to bees buzz, hugging a sheep, throwing rocks, seeing how close I could get to a squirrel, and talking to the dog. I shared communion with nature and my very special five-year-old nephew, D. J.

D. J. likes to come to the ranch for a visit, and every time he does, I learn something important. He is from a big city where the ecologists live in twenty-story condominiums and tell us how to manage what they call "open space," as if nobody lives there. D. J. comes from the land of manicured lawns where the only Lions, Moose, or Elk are in men's clubs, or in a zoo. I feel sorry for city kids whose only experience with mud pies is on a dessert plate in a restaurant.

79

D. J. says he wants to be a veterinarian when he grows up, and in preparation for his latest visit to the ranch, someone had given him a jar that was supposed to be good for catching and studying bugs and other small animals. It had a plastic leaf in it and was just like the old Mason jars that I used as a kid for the same purpose, only D. J.'s probably cost twelve dollars. I thought it might be neat for us to catch a frog for D. J. to put in his jar and take back to nursery school for show and tell. They had probably never seen a real frog before.

"Hoppy" the frog stayed in his jar overnight, but the next day, D. J. wanted to turn him loose because "he looked so sad in the jar." So D. J. turned him loose in the house for my nervous wife to discover later. Then it was my wife's turn to look sad. Next we caught a mad honeybee. My five-year-old environmentalist nephew set it free in the enclosed space of the truck cab as we were driving down the road.

At five years of age, D. J. had already discovered that if you tried to tame nature you only ended up destroying it.

At lunch, D. J.'s food disappeared into his pockets. Later I found him trying to feed his burger to my horse, Gentleman, his crust to the birds who roost in the barn rafters, and his French fries to the squirrels.

D. J. doesn't know yet about acid rain, melting ice caps, aerosols destroying the ozone, or disappearing forests that ecologists write 700-page books about. He does know that plants still grow up and roots grow down. Bees still buzz, grass still grows, and frogs can be hard to catch. (Just ask my wife.) One very special day last week, I discovered once again what every five year old knows. All is well with nature, it is just us grown-ups that are out of balance. If we covered the earth with concrete, grass would still grow up through the cracks.

Since D. J.'s visit, I don't mind it so much that a little dirt falls in my face from a bird's nest overhead when I close the shop door, that the deer eat my hedge, or that the raccoons dig for worms in my lawn. I actually took some time yesterday to watch some quail scratch in the dirt and to smile back at the cat.

HOPEWELL

TODAY I AM WALKING the grassy slopes of the Hopewell Cemetery near the town of what used to be Huckaby. I have never been here before in my life, although five generations of my family are planted in this good Missouri soil.

I am walking with a man whose name is spelled the same as mine, and I have never met another Lee Pitts before. It's kind of nice. This day I am suffering from the same depression of moral spirit as the rest of the country. Back home in California, the policemen who beat Rodney King have just been found innocent. People are rioting in the streets, burning buildings, and looting stores because they feel hopeless—trapped in a world with no future. Gloom and doom pervades the national psyche. Can't we all just get along?

As I walk through the Hopewell Cemetery, I begin to read the headstones. Next to the graves of my great-great-great-grandparents are three of their children. My namesake tells me that one child died at the age of one year when a bucket of boiling water fell on him. A pair of twins both died the same year from a disease, probably whooping cough. In fact, the cemetery is filled with children who died from simple things like the flu. Tuberculosis killed twice as many people as car wrecks, but that was because only one in five people living just fifty years ago owned a car. One in seven had a phone, and one-third didn't even have indoor plumbing. Yet none of these people ever protested their plight by burning down the one grocery store within miles of their homes, and the thought of shooting the firemen who tried to put out a fire is unthinkable to God-fearing country folks.

The headstones tell the story—life never was easy.

Young people today are upset that they can't afford the down payment on a house. Over half of the farmers buried here in Hopewell never owned their own land, yet they didn't drag a truck driver out of his cab and beat him near to death. Three-fourths of the adults buried here fifty years ago never graduated from high school and never made more than $1,000 a year, but they didn't torch their town. The women buried here didn't rise up in arms when it was suggested that the unemployment problem could be eliminated if the ten million working women would just quit their jobs.

I understand the despair felt by black people in this country today, but fifty years ago they could not even be buried in this cemetery. They could not drink out of the same water fountain, go to the same bomb shelter, or be seen engaging in a biracial handshake. A black woman was able to buy a dress in the white-owned store but she couldn't try it on first. We have made some progress the past fifty years, I think. Admittedly, not fast enough.

These good country folks buried here had reason to give up, and some did. Fifty years ago it was dust storms, not smoke from smoldering fires, that forced many to flee on flatbed trucks to the land of milk and honey—wherever that was. Some people stayed put, and I observe this day that they are infinitely happier than those who left. These good country folks simply cannot understand why people would burn their own town to the ground. The actions of those who have packed our nation's cities to over-flowing are alien to them. These people knew despair, too, but they kept trying. There has always been hope in the heartland.

This day as I walk between headstones, I am struck by an-other curiosity. Many of the country folks who left for the bright lights of the big city have come back to Hopewell to be buried on this hill next to a cow pasture where the birds sing and the wind whistles through the trees. Even if you were one of the two mil-lion members of Hoboes of America that roamed the country fifty years ago, you were still somebody in Hopewell. You were still entitled to a tombstone and a free plot of ground to rest your weary head.

As I leave the cemetery, I am struck by the irony of one epi-taph. I think it goes to the heart of America's problems and her collective despair. It says simply, "He never should have left home."

DAYLIGHT SAVINGS:
IT'S ABOUT TIME

WE AREN'T SO SMART! I have always heard that humans are superior to animals because we are able to reason. We are rational. I ask you, is daylight savings time the act of a rational being? Any idea that makes the work day last an hour longer is not a good idea!

You won't catch farm animals springing forward or falling back. They know what time it is without a Rolex or a Timex. Shockproof and waterproof, the animal's biological clock keeps right on ticking.

I always know what time it is by how my animals are behaving. My dog, Aussie, always barks one half hour before I want to get up. Sheep may be stupid but they know that the time after lunch was meant for napping. The pig spends 40 percent of his time resting and the rest of his time eating. I can't think of a better way to pass the time than that. Can you?

At half past four every day, my cattle wander down to the water trough for a drink—sort of a cow cocktail hour. The way I figure it, Mother Nature intended for that "happy hour" of the day to be spent in serious drinking. And who am I to argue with Mother Nature?

I think that cattle have the best built-in clocks. They only break out of their pasture when it's starting to get dark and their keeper can't see to gather them in, and they always know when it's feeding time. What time is it? It's half past feeding time. You can set your watch by it.

Clocks and watches were invented by city folk so they would know when to take a coffee break, when to eat, and when to quit. Just think, if you didn't have clocks and watches, you could never be late!

Country folks don't need clocks, they have roosters. Country people know that at daybreak they rise with the rooster and at sunset they should be engaged in something to crow about. Wives also have built-in clocks. They always know what time it is. "It's time to take out the trash. It's time to do the dishes. It's time to mow the lawn." It's always time for something!

I heard a guy the other day say, "I sure like the days better with daylight savings." How crazy—it's still the same twenty-four hours, isn't it? They aren't fooling anyone. My pickup still won't start till eight o'clock in the morning.

Daylight savings doesn't make the day any longer, it just makes you feel like the day's longer. I went back to the house the first night of daylight savings at half past six and spent the rest of the evening trying to figure out what to do with my "extra" time. The switch in time gave me insomnia so bad, I couldn't even sleep when it was time to get up the next morning.

We put too much emphasis on what time it is. We live by the clock too much. Who cares what time it is? In the country it stays light till it gets dark anyway.

WHEN I WAS YOUR AGE

HAPPINESS TODAY IS having a large, caring and loving family . . . that lives far, far away. But it wasn't that way when I was your age. Back then, if my mother needed a place to send me after school, it was to my grandparents' house, not to a day-care center. If you looked up a person's name in our phone book, it was a little confusing because for every last name there was a John, a Johnny, and a Johnny, Jr.—three generations all living in the same neighborhood. A phone call to a "distant" relative was not even long distance, and you didn't need an appointment to stop by and visit an uncle, an aunt, a brother, or a sister. Close relatives really were—sometimes right next door.

Sundays were for pot roasts and family get-togethers, and there were just as many people over on Monday to eat the leftovers. Christmas and Thanksgiving were mandatory family affairs but so were birthdays and anniversaries.

When I was your age, we didn't know anything about Alzheimer's disease. We just thought grandma was getting a little senile, so we all took turns taking care of her. It was no big deal. When grandpa fell and broke his hip, he couldn't get any rest for all the friends and relatives that showed up and offered to help.

Nowadays when a young person wants to spend a week's vacation with his parents, he probably has to be shipped off, boarding a plane with a name tag around his neck to visit a divorced parent in a faraway city. It scares me that city kids have to join violent gangs to feel wanted, as if wearing the same color uniform can replace the family feeling. When I was your age, the only gangs I joined were the Little League and the Cub Scouts. Family members filled the bleachers on game day and for a Scout-A-Rama. They bought my sister's Girl Scout cookies and paid me fifty cents to mow their lawns each week.

That was when I was your age—but now I am my age, and like the rest of the baby-boom generation I moved away from home. Just like the brother who left the farm or the sister who moved to the big city, I forsook my roots in search of fame and fortune. Didn't we all? A person will do almost anything for money it seems. Today, the four members of my immediate family live in four different states. We see each other maybe once a year, probably at a funeral.

Though I have a great wife, a nice home, and a moderately successful career, I am at that stage in my life when I feel like I am missing something. I didn't know what it was until I went back home recently.

I miss my family. I think my whole generation does.

As baby boomers, we have bigger homes and more cars than our parents did, and yet we are not as rich. A Navajo Indian once told me that you can't get rich if you have taken care of your family properly. That's what worries me. Who will take care of our generation?

As the baby boomers get older, it will be the parents who are the orphans. We cannot expect our good friend "what's his name" who moved in next door to be our caretaker. He's got the same problem. We will probably be cataloged in rest homes and forgotten in retirement communities and ghettos for the elderly, unable to reminisce with nurses we never knew. I imagine it will be lonely out there, growing old and hating it. We have pursued the American dream with gusto but forgot to bring our families along for the trip.

A lady far smarter than I gave a speech to a group of college women a few years back. Her speech raised quite a ruckus at the time because she was a traditional kind of woman and the Wellesley students were not. I only hope those unruly students listened. Barbara Bush told those young ladies, "At the end of your life, you will never regret not having passed one more test, not winning one more verdict, or not closing one more deal. You will regret time not spent with a husband, a child, a friend, or a parent."

She's right, you know . . .

When the Trashman Comes Early

DO YOU EVER THINK about all the wrecks that never happened? Of course not. It is only when disaster occurs that we think of the importance of an employee. The head honchos of Exxon probably never heard of the captain of the Exxon Valdez until he allegedly spent the afternoon in a bar taking on fluids and the evening disgorging them. Those drinks brought one of the world's largest companies to its knees, costing them about a billion dollars a drink, I believe.

Speaking of drinks, a few years ago the Perrier Company of France also found out the hard way about the power of people. It is now speculated that a single employee cleaned Perrier's water filters with a toxic substance called benzene instead of the usual cleaner and that simple mistake cost the company their reputation and forty million dollars.

AT&T customers had a hard time reaching out and touching someone a few years back because a single technician forgot to program some information into a computer. People couldn't get through, AT&T was embarrassed on national television, and MCI and Sprint got some new customers—all because of a single individual. That one person had a bigger effect on AT&T's bottom line that year than the chairman of the board.

Conglomerates today are run by committees, task forces, and consensus, but it is the person at the counter or the driver of the truck who is often the image of each company. That is why the world will never be taken over by the junk-bond kings. McDonalds may have fancy ads on television, but if the kids waiting on you at the counter are rude, nobody will come back. If the pump jockey at the local station fills your gas tank with "Diesel" instead of "Regular," you won't believe Exxon when they say that the situation in Alaska is "environmentally stabilized."

Frequently our impressions of a company are formed by just one employee out of 12,000. A good example was brought to mind recently on a local television show. A trash-disposal firm was trying to get the county's okay for a new landfill near a small town. All the city fathers were against it, but finally it went before the townspeople in a referendum. Much to everyone's surprise, the referendum passed and the landfill was approved.

When a little old lady was asked by a reporter why she voted for the referendum, she replied, "Because my trashman always comes early and on time. I figure it's a responsible company."

Ah, the power of the person!

I was thinking about why I deal with certain businesses in the area, and it almost always came down to a single person. I buy my farm supplies from a firm because once I ordered some heavy panels from them and a nice young man not only delivered them but helped me put them in place, too. I go back to a local fast-food joint because one time I accidentally knocked a Coke out of the hand of a waitress there and she insisted it was her fault. It wasn't, but I liked the fact that she tried to make me feel not quite so foolish.

I buy my cars from a nice man largely because when I take my car in to get it serviced, he also washes it for me. I patronize a white tablecloth restaurant because the waiter always remembers my name and knows how I like my steak.

So here's to the company truck driver who stops and helps a lady fix a flat, and here's to the garbage man who is always on time. Here's to the cowboy who always leaves a gate as he found it. Here's to the newspaper boy who doesn't throw your paper on the roof. Here's to the baker who gives you a baker's dozen, to the clerk who gives you a smile, and to the farmer who is careful with chemicals.

Thank goodness for the insults that were never spoken, the gates that were closed, the doors that were opened, and all the wrecks that never happened.

And here's to the people who know the power of the person.

Come Home

I MUST CONFESS THAT I once got in trouble for bringing water balloons to school. Now the kids bring magnums and assault rifles. I remember the big scandal one year at our high school when a senior girl was said to be in "the family way." Whisper, whisper, whisper. Nowadays many high school students have school-aged children of their own before they get their high school diploma.

We got in trouble for talking in class, while today's students arrange drug deals in the back of the classroom. Our agriculture teacher kept order by paddling a few behinds. These days he'd be charged with child abuse. We used to get in trouble for running in the halls, but today's students may actually be running for their lives.

There is a way to solve the crime crises, the drug dilemma, the welfare mess, and the lack of literacy without throwing more tax money at these problems. The answer is very simple and can be summed up in just two words. The same two words the neighbor lady used to yell at me after I had only been at her house for twenty minutes—*go home.* All animals have a homing instinct, but in people it seems to have gone dormant. In the computer age, our wiring somehow got disconnected and we forgot where home is.

We have all heard remarkable stories of a dog being lost on the East Coast when the family went on vacation only to show up months later on the front doorstep clear across the continent. I have read of old-timers driving horses 600 miles from home to a new ranch, but when spring came, the mares had traveled back to their home grounds to foal. Turtles, alligators, and salmon go back to where they were born to have their own children. A frightened calf or a fawn will run back to the spot where its mother last left it. Despite being just a few days old, they have a remarkable sense of direction—a sense of direction that humans seem to have lost.

It is time for the people of this country to revert back to our animal instincts and go home again. For the divorced parents of a dysfunctional family or the shiftless father with a "Will work for food" sign in his hand, it means going home to the unwed mother and fatherless children and creating a warm and loving atmosphere so that the children aren't forced to find love in gangs and drugs.

When members of the "lost generation" become frightened like a newborn calf, they don't run for home anymore. Far too often it is the mother on drugs or the abusive father doing the frightening. Today's kids are raised at day care and on fast food. Instead, they need a home where "Saturday Night Special" refers to what's for dinner rather than something you take to school for protection.

This problem of being lost with no sense of direction is not just a problem with our young people. It used to be that it was the responsibility of the child to take care of the parents when the roles were reversed. Instead, today's elderly are shipped off to institutions. We call it a "home" to ease our consciences, but it is not really home. You'll see what I mean when it is your turn. I'm glad my mom didn't send me to an institution when I was a child just because I couldn't feed myself and occasionally wet the bed.

The problems in our schools, in our cities, and with our country is that we have lost our sense of direction—and when the scared run for safety, the lights are out, the doors are locked, and there is nobody home.

Rest in Peace

I CAN'T RECALL WHAT famous author wrote the lines "It was the best of times. It was the worst of times," but he or she could have been referring to a time in this country that we know as The Great Depression. Those who lived through it will tell you there was nothing great about it.

Like always, good times preceded the crash. Prices for farm goods were soaring, thanks to a seemingly endless export market for the product of the farmer's toil. So, farmers did what farmers always do whenever they get a little extra change in their pockets. They bought more land at higher prices. To farm the land, they bought newer and bigger machinery and paid for it like farmers always do—on the installment plan.

Then, almost overnight, demand dried up like a withering fruit. America's farmers and ranchers had managed to overproduce themselves out of prosperity once again. Naturally, prices plummeted, as prices always do. The men and women of the land were left with high-priced land and machinery payments. Land prices fell and so did many rural banks. How many times, I wonder, has the familiar boom-and-bust cycle of agriculture repeated itself?

During that time we now simply refer to as "the depression," a Missouri farmer, the son of an original homesteader, planted a corn crop for his family. But the howling wind that came from across the plains dried up his corn and his family's future. The blowing dust made housewives crazy and children sickly. Insanity was about all that would grow in the dust of the depression, irrigated only by sweat and tears.

Faced with the unceasing winds, some farmers in this part of the country planted fast-growing windbreaks, almost as an afterthought. But not our Missouri homesteader—no, he planted a tree. Not a tree really, just a twig—a cutting from a dying matriarch. That Missouri farmer carried water to that twig from the well his father had dug by hand when this homestead was settled. There was precious little water in those days, but the farmer gave that baby oak what little there was to spare.

To some of his Missouri neighbors, planting the tree was the act of a lunatic. The dirt and the wind perhaps had taken yet another victim. After all, trees grow slowly and the farmer would be long gone before that tiny twig grew into a giant oak.

But as was the custom of those sturdy Midwestern farmers, this tree was not planted for his generation to enjoy. It was planted for the farmer's children and his children's children. He planted corn for himself and a tree for posterity.

To most everyone's disbelief, that oak tree eventually sent down scraggly roots into the parched ground, surviving harsh winters and hot summers. Moles burrowed under it, insects and diseases assaulted it, and wind and ice tried to kill it. In this land of few oak trees, that tree became somewhat of a symbol. The first leaves that sprouted were a victory for hope. America's heartland would survive.

Funny thing, those windbreaks that the farmers planted in desperation are now thickets that have to be cleared away with modern herbicides and powerful tractors. Darn those worthless bushes anyway.

If you would travel back to southwest Missouri today, you would probably find that tree. Only now it is no longer a twig but a giant oak. Beneath that tree is a family burial plot. That tree, which was planted in the depths of depression, now shades the farmer who planted it. He will be shaded from the sun and the rain for as long as the tree shall live. Finally, the farmer has his reward for planting a tree instead of a thicket.

This Missouri story is often retold in the "old country" of my ancestors, and it comes to my mind whenever I pass a modern cemetery. I pause and wonder: When our children and our children's children walk through the cemetery where we are buried, do we want them to fight through thickets and thorns that were planted as quick-and-easy answers to the complex problems of our generation? Or do we want them to stand under a sturdy tree in quiet appreciation? Will our headstones be shrouded by thickets and thorns, or will they clearly state that we came and we sowed so that our children could reap?

THESE THINGS I WISH

WE'VE ALL BEEN TOLD by our parents or grandparents how they walked or rode their horses six miles uphill to school in the snow and then six miles uphill to come home. During the depression, there was no coasting on the downhill, so it was understandable that the Cornhuskers, the Okies, and the prune pickers wanted things to be better for their kids and grandkids. For most folks that meant uprooting their family from the country and attempting to send down roots through the concrete of the big city. Along with this new way of life came a new way of looking at things. That old jalopy that carried the hopes and dreams of entire families out of the dust bowl now has a bumper sticker on it that reads, "He who dies with the most toys wins."

Personally, I want more than that for America's young future. I want them to have hand-me-down clothes, homemade ice cream, and leftover meat loaf, just like I had.

For the good of our country and our children, these things I wish for you . . .

I hope someday you know the love of a pony and the pain of saddle sores. May you learn to appreciate the magic of a firefly and the majesty of a mountain.

I truly wish nobody gives you a brand-new car when you turn sixteen, and I hope you have a job by then. I hope your parents insist that you wash the dishes, make your bed, and mow the lawn.

I wish for you the chance to see a baby calf or colt be born and to see your old dog put to sleep. I hope you get a black eye fighting for something you believe in.

I hope you have to share a bedroom with your younger brother or sister. Sure, it's all right to draw a line down the middle of the room indicating your half of the space, but when they want to crawl under the covers at night with you because they are scared, I hope you'll let them.

I hope you have to walk uphill to school with your friends and that you live in a town where you can do so safely. On rainy days I hope you have to hitch a ride with your mom, and I hope she doesn't have to drop you off two blocks away so you won't be seen riding with someone as "uncool" as your mother.

If you want a slingshot, I hope that your mother doesn't just fork over the money and that your father is around to teach you how to make one. I hope that you learn to entertain yourself early in life by digging in the dirt or reading a good book.

Here's hoping you discover how glorious that church can make a Sunday. May you experience that feel-good emotion of putting part of your allowance in the collection plate and of singing hymns off-key at the top of your voice.

I hope you learn humility by getting humiliated and that you find out about honesty by getting cheated. May you learn to vacuum the carpet, wash the car, and change the oil. I sure hope you go to college but not if it's just to avoid the real world.

I trust you will learn how to use those newfangled computers, but I hope you don't forget to learn how to add and subtract in your head. I don't care what you want to be when you grow up, but if you want to be a doctor, I hope it's not just because they make a lot of money.

I hope you get teased by your friends when you have your first crush on a girl. When you talk back to your mother, I hope you learn what soap tastes like.

May you skin your knee climbing a mountain and burn your hand on the stove. May you get beat when you compete and may you never experience an undefeated season. Win or lose, may you look forward to the next competition.

I hope that you get trapped in a smoke-filled room and you get sick when some stupid person blows cigarette smoke in your face. I don't care if you try a beer once, but I sure hope you don't like it too much. If your friends offer you a joint or some dope, I hope you are smart enough to realize that they are not your friends.

I sure hope that you take the time to sit on a porch with your grandpa or to go fishing with your uncle. May you feel sorrow at a funeral and know the real meaning of Christmas. I hope your mother punishes you when you throw a baseball through the neighbor's plate-glass window, but I hope she hugs you and gives you a kiss when you bring her a plaster-of-paris mold of your handprint for Christmas.

May you laugh at the rodeo clown, cry when it hurts, and swell with pride at the sight of Old Glory. I hope to see you some day in a Fourth of July parade.

These things I wish for you—tough times, disappointment, hard work, and most of all . . . love.

ABOUT THE AUTHOR

LEE PITTS IS THE executive editor for *Livestock Market Digest,* a weekly newspaper serving the livestock industry. He is the author of five previous books and a syndicated weekly humor column. His is a recognized byline in rural weekly newspapers and monthly magazines throughout the West. Pitts is also the author and narrator of the full-length feature video *From a Western Point of View.*

Lee Pitts has spent the last two decades traveling around rural America writing stories and speaking about agricultural issues and the agrarian way of life. When he is not busy traveling down dirt roads, he makes his home in Los Osos, California, with his wife, Diane.